German Dialogues for Beginners
Book 2

Over 100 Daily Used Phrases and Short Stories to Learn German in Your Car. Have Fun and Grow Your Vocabulary with Crazy Effective Language Learning Lessons

www.LearnLikeNatives.com

www.LearnLikeNatives.com

© Copyright 2020
By Learn Like A Native

ALL RIGHTS RESERVED

No part of this book may be reproduced, stored in a retrieval system, or transmitted in any form or by any means, without the prior written permission of the publisher.

www.LearnLikeNatives.com

TABLE OF CONTENT

INTRODUCTION	5
CHAPTER 1 John's Homework / School + Classroom	17
Translation of the Story	31
John's Homework	31
CHAPTER 2 Thrift Store Bargain / house and furniture	39
Translation of the Story	53
Thrift Store Bargain	53
CHAPTER 3 The Goat / common present tense verbs	61
Translation of the Story	77
The Goat	77
CONCLUSION	87
About the Author	93

www.LearnLikeNatives.com

www.LearnLikeNatives.com

INTRODUCTION

Before we dive into some German, I want to congratulate you, whether you're just beginning, continuing, or resuming your language learning journey. Here at Learn Like a Native, we understand the determination it takes to pick up a new language and after reading this book, you'll be another step closer to achieving your language goals.

As a thank you for learning with us, we are giving you free access to our 'Speak Like a Native' eBook. It's packed full of practical advice and insider tips on how to make language learning quick, easy, and most importantly, enjoyable. Head over to LearnLikeNatives.com to access your free guide and peruse our huge selection of language learning resources.

Learning a new language is a bit like cooking—you need several different ingredients and the right technique, but the end result is sure to be delicious. We created this book of short stories for learning German because language is alive. Language is about the senses—hearing, tasting the words on your tongue, and touching another culture up close. Learning a language in a classroom is a fine place to start, but it's not a complete introduction to a language.

In this book, you'll find a language come to life. These short stories are miniature immersions into the German language, at a level that is perfect for beginners. This book is not a lecture on grammar. It's not an endless vocabulary list. This book is the closest you can come to a language immersion without leaving the country. In the stories within, you will see people speaking to each other, going through daily life situations, and using the most common, helpful words and phrases in language.

www.LearnLikeNatives.com

You are holding the key to bringing your German studies to life.

Made for Beginners

We made this book with beginners in mind. You'll find that the language is simple, but not boring. Most of the book is in the present tense, so you will be able to focus on dialogues, root verbs, and understand and find patterns in subject-verb agreement.

This is not "just" a translated book. While reading novels and short stories translated into German is a wonderful thing, beginners (and even novices) often run into difficulty. Literary licenses and complex sentence structure can make reading in your second language truly difficult—not to mention BORING. That's why German Short Stories for Beginners is the perfect book to pick up. The stories are simple, but not infantile. They were not written for children, but the language is simple so that beginners can pick it up.

The Benefits of Learning a Second Language

If you have picked up this book, it's likely that you are already aware of the many benefits of learning a second language. Besides just being fun, knowing more than one language opens up a whole new world to you. You will be able to communicate with a much larger chunk of the world. Opportunities in the workforce will open up, and maybe even your day-to-day work will be improved. Improved communication can also help you expand your business. And from a neurological perspective, learning a second language is like taking your daily vitamins and eating well, for your brain!

www.LearnLikeNatives.com

How To Use The Book

The chapters of this book all follow the same structure:

- A short story with several dialogs
- A summary in German
- A list of important words and phrases and their English translation
- Questions to test your understanding
- Answers to check if you were right
- The English translation of the story to clear every doubt

You may use this book however is comfortable for you, but we have a few recommendations for getting the most out of the experience. Try these tips and if they work for you, you can use them on every chapter throughout the book.

www.LearnLikeNatives.com

1) Start by reading the story all the way through. Don't stop or get hung up on any particular words or phrases. See how much of the plot you can understand in this way. We think you'll get a lot more of it than you may expect, but it is completely normal not to understand everything in the story. You are learning a new language, and that takes time.

2) Read the summary in German. See if it matches what you have understood of the plot.

3) Read the story through again, slower this time. See if you can pick up the meaning of any words or phrases you don't understand by using context clues and the information from the summary.

4) Test yourself! Try to answer the five comprehension questions that come at the end of each story. Write your answers

down, and then check them against the answer key. How did you do? If you didn't get them all, no worries!

5) Look over the vocabulary list that accompanies the chapter. Are any of these the words you did not understand? Did you already know the meaning of some of them from your reading?

6) Now go through the story once more. Pay attention this time to the words and phrases you haven't understand. If you'd like, take the time to look them up to expand your meaning of the story. Every time you read over the story, you'll understand more and more.

7) Move on to the next chapter when you are ready.

www.LearnLikeNatives.com

Read and Listen

The audio version is the best way to experience this book, as you will hear a native German speaker tell you each story. You will become accustomed to their accent as you listen along, a huge plus for when you want to apply your new language skills in the real world.

If this has ignited your language learning passion and you are keen to find out what other resources are available, go to **LearnLikeNatives.com**, where you can access our vast range of free learning materials. Don't know where to begin? An excellent place to start is our 'Speak Like a Native' free eBook, full of practical advice and insider tips on how to make language learning quick, easy, and most importantly, enjoyable.

And remember, small steps add up to great advancements! No moment is better to begin learning than the present.

www.LearnLikeNatives.com

FREE BOOK!

Get the *FREE BOOK* that reveals the secrets path to learn any language fast, and without leaving your country.

Discover:

- The **language 5 golden rules** to master languages at will

- Proven **mind training techniques** to revolutionize your learning

- A complete step-by-step guide to **conquering any language**

www.LearnLikeNatives.com

www.LearnLikeNatives.com

www.LearnLikeNatives.com

CHAPTER 1
John's Homework / School + Classroom

HANDLUNG

Frau Kloss ist **Lehrerin** der 4. Klasse. Sie unterrichtet an der Homewood Grundschule. Die **Schule** befindet sich in einem roten Backsteingebäude. Es ist in einer Kleinstadt.

Frau Kloss hat eine Klasse von 15 Schülern. Ihre **Schüler** sind Jungen und Mädchen. Sie sind normalerweise gute Schüler. Frau Kloss hat eine Routine. Ihre Schüler beginnen den Tag an ihren **Pulten**, in ihren **Stühlen** sitzend. Frau Kloss ruft zum Appell auf.

"Louise?" sagt sie.

"Hier!" ruft Louise.

"Mike?" sagt Frau Kloss.

"Anwesend", sagt Mike.

"John?" sagt Frau Kloss.

"Hier, Frau Kloss", sagt John.

Und so beginnt Frau Kloss nach dem Appell den Tag mit **Mathe**. Für ihre Schüler ist Mathe schwierig. Die Klasse hört Frau Kloss beim unterrichten zu. Sie sehen, wie sie auf die **Tafel** schreibt. Manchmal löst ein Schüler ein Problem vor der Klasse. Sie verwenden **Kreide**, um die Lösung aufzuschreiben. Die anderen Schüler lösen die Probleme in ihren **Heften**.

Jedermanns Lieblingszeit ist die Mittagszeit. Die Klasse geht in den Speisesaal. Sie haben zwei Möglichkeiten: Eine Möglichkeit ist eine gesunde Mahlzeit aus Fleisch und Gemüse. Die andere Möglichkeit ist Pizza oder Hamburger, einige Schüler bringen ein Mittagessen von zu Hause mit.

Am Nachmittag lernen sie **Geschichte**. Freitags haben sie Natur**wissenschaften** im **Labor**. Sie machen **Experimente**, wie das Züchten von Pflanzen aus einem Stück Kartoffel.

Frau Kloss gibt ihren Schülern jeden Tag **Hausaufgaben**. Sie nehmen die Aufgaben mit nach Hause, sie lernen abends. Am nächsten Tag bringen sie die Hausaufgaben zur Schule. Die einzige Entschuldigung für unvollständige Hausaufgaben ist eine Mitteilung von den Eltern.

Eines Tages bespricht die Klasse die **Englisch** Hausaufgaben gemeinsam.

"An alle, bringt bitte eure **Unterlagen** an meinen Schreibtisch", sagt Frau Kloss. Jeder bringt seine Hausaufgaben zu Frau Kloss. Alle außer John.

"John, wo ist deine Hausaufgabe?" fragt Frau Kloss.

Johns Gesicht ist sehr rot, er ist nervös.

"Ich habe sie nicht", sagt John.

"Hast du eine Entschuldigung von deinen Eltern?" fragt Frau Kloss.

"Nein", sagt John.

"Warum hast du deine Hausaufgaben nicht gemacht?" fragt Frau Kloss. John sagt etwas sehr leise.

"Was? Wir können dich nicht hören", sagt Frau Kloss. Sie schenkt John ein freundliches Lächeln. Er wirkt nervös.

"Mein Hund hat meine Hausaufgaben gefressen", sagt John. Frau Kloss und die anderen Schüler lachen. Diese Begründung ist die typischste Ausrede dafür, Arbeit nicht erledigt zu haben.

"Ist sie in deinem **Rucksack**? Oder vielleicht dein **Spind**?" fragt Frau Kloss. Sie will John helfen.

"Nein, mein Hund hat sie gefressen!" behauptet John.

"Das ist die **älteste Ausrede der Welt**", sagt Frau Kloss.

"Es ist wahr!" sagt John. John ist ein guter Schüler. Normalerweise schreibt er **glatte Einsen**. Frau Kloss will John nicht ins **Rektorzimmer** schicken, weil er gelogen hat. Sie glaubt John nicht, aber sie beschließt, ihm eine weitere Chance zu geben.

"Bring die Hausaufgaben morgen", sagt Frau Kloss. "Hier ist eine weitere Kopie." John nimmt die **Arbeitsblätter** und dankt Frau Kloss. Die

Klasse wendet sich ihren **Kunst**heften zu. Heute zeichnen sie im Kunstunterricht ein Bild mit Bunt**stiften**. Die Schüler lieben den Kunstunterricht. Es ist eine Chance zu entspannen. Sie zeichnen und zeichnen, bis die **Klingel** läutet. Die Schule ist vorbei.

Die Schüler sprechen in den Gängen. Sie tauschen Notizen aus. Die Schüler der 4. Klasse warten draußen. Ihre Eltern holen sie ab. Einige von ihnen sind zu Fuß unterwegs. Manche von ihnen sind mit Autos gekommen. Die Lehrer helfen ihnen, ihre Eltern zu finden.

Frau Kloss beendet ihre Arbeit. Sie packt ihren **Laptop** in ihre Tasche. Ihr Klassenzimmer ist sauber und leer. Sie geht nach draußen. Als sie zu ihrem Auto geht, sieht sie John und seinen Vater. Johns Vater holt ihn mit seinem Hund ab. Frau Kloss winkt John und seinem Vater zu.

"Hallo, John!" sagt Frau Kloss.

"Guten Tag, Frau Kloss", sagt John.

"Ist das der Hund, der deine Hausaufgaben gefressen hat?" fragt Frau Kloss. Sie lächelt, damit John weiß, dass sie scherzt.

"Ja, Frau Kloss", sagt Johns Vater. "Danke für Ihr Verständnis, John macht sich solche Sorgen, Ärger zu bekommen!"

Frau Kloss ist verblüfft! Diesmal hat der Hund wirklich die Hausaufgaben gefressen.

VOKABELLISTE

Lehrer	teacher

www.LearnLikeNatives.com

Schule	school
Klasse	class
Schüler	students
Pult	desk
Stuhl	chair
Appell	roll call
Mathe	math
Tafel	blackboard
Kreide	chalk
Heft	notebook
Geschichte	history
Wissenschaft	science
Labor	lab
Experiment	experiment
Hausaufgabe	homework
Englisch	English

Unterlagen	papers
Rucksack	backpack
Spind	locker
die älteste Ausrede der Welt	the oldest excuse in the book
glatte Einsen	straight A's
Rektorzimmer	principal's office
Arbeitsblätter	worksheet
Stifte	pencils
Klingel	bell
Laptop	laptop

FRAGEN

1) Wie beginnt der Tag in Frau Kloss' Klasse?

    a) die Schüler stehen und rufen

    b) mit einer Hausaufgabe

    c) Appell

    d) Frau Kloss ruft

2) Was ist die Lieblingstageszeit aller an der Homewood Grundschule?

    a) Appell

    b) Mittagszeit

    c) Matheunterricht

    d) nachdem die Klingel läutet

3) Warum sagt Frau Kloss, dass Johns Entschuldigung die älteste auf der Welt ist?

a) weil jeder diese Ausrede nutzt

b) John der älteste in der Klasse ist

c) weil die Welt rund ist

d) sein Hund sieben Jahre alt ist

4) Was muss man haben, wenn man seine Hausaufgaben nicht macht?

a) ein wissenschaftliches Experiment

b) eine gute Entschuldigung

c) nichts, es ist in Ordnung

d) eine Mitteilung der Eltern

5) Warum ist Frau Kloss am Ende der Geschichte überrascht?

a) sie erkennt, dass John die Wahrheit sagte

b) Johns Hund ist eigentlich ein Pferd

c) John spricht nicht mit ihr

d) Johns Vater sieht aus wie John

ANTWORTEN

1) Wie beginnt der Tag in Frau Kloss' Klasse?

    c) Appell

2) Was ist die Lieblingstageszeit aller an der Homewood Grundschule?

    b) Mittagszeit

3) Warum sagt Frau Kloss, dass Johns Entschuldigung die älteste der Welt ist?

a) weil jeder diese Entschuldigung nutzt

4) Was muss man haben, wenn man seine Hausaufgaben nicht macht?

d) eine Mitteilung der Eltern

5) Warum ist Frau Kloss am Ende der Geschichte überrascht?

a) sie erkennt, dass John die Wahrheit sagte

www.LearnLikeNatives.com

Translation of the Story

John's Homework

STORY

Mrs. Kloss is a grade 4 **teacher**. She teaches at Homewood Elementary School. The **school** is in a red brick building. It is in a small town.

Mrs. Kloss has a **class** of 15 students. Her **students** are boys and girls. They are usually good students. Mrs. Kloss has a routine. Her students start the day at their **desks**, seated in their **chairs**. Mrs. Kloss calls **roll call**.

"Louise?" she says.

"Here!" shouts Louise.

"Mike?" says Mrs. Kloss.

"Present," says Mike.

"John?"

"Here, Mrs. Kloss," John says.

And so on. After roll call, Mrs. Kloss starts the day with **math**. For her students, math is difficult. The class listens to Mrs. Kloss teach. They watch as she writes on the **blackboard**. Sometimes, one student solves a problem in front of the class. They use **chalk** to write out the solution. The other students do the problems in their **notebooks**.

Everyone's favorite time is lunch time. The class goes to the lunchroom. They have two choices. One choice is a healthy meal of meat and vegetables. The other choice is pizza or hamburgers. Some students bring a lunch from home.

In the afternoon, they study **history**. On Fridays, they have **science** class in the **lab**. They do **experiments**, like growing plants from a piece of potato.

Mrs. Kloss gives her students **homework** every day. They take the work home. They work at night. The next day, they bring it to school. The only excuse for incomplete homework is a note from their parents.

One day, the class reviews the **English** homework together.

"Everyone, please bring your **papers** to my desk," says Mrs. Kloss. Everyone brings their homework to Mrs. Kloss. Everyone except for John.

"John, where is your homework?" says Mrs. Kloss.

John's face is very red. He is nervous.

"I don't have it," says John.

"Do you have a note from your parents?" asks Mrs. Kloss.

"No," says John.

"Why didn't you do your homework, then?" asks Mrs. Kloss. John says something very quietly.

"What? We can't hear you," says Mrs. Kloss. She gives John a kind smile. He looks nervous.

"My dog ate my homework," says John. Mrs. Kloss and the other students laugh. This excuse is the most typical excuse for not having work done.

"Is it in your **backpack**? Or maybe your **locker**?" asks Mrs. Kloss. She wants to help John.

"No, my dog ate it!" insists John.

"That's the **oldest excuse in the book**," says Mrs. Kloss.

"It is true!" says John. John is a good student. He usually makes **straight A's**. Mrs. Kloss does not want to send Jon to the **principal's office** for lying. She does not believe John, but she decides to give him another chance.

"Bring the homework tomorrow," says Mrs. Kloss. "Here is another copy." John takes the **worksheet** and thanks Mrs. Kloss. The class turns to their **art** notebook. Today in art class they are drawing a picture with colored **pencils**. Students love art class. It is a chance to relax. They draw and draw until the **bell** rings. School is over.

Students talk in the hallways. They exchange notes. The Grade 4 students wait outside. Their parents pick them up. Some of them are on foot. Some of them are in cars. The teachers help them to find their parents.

Mrs. Kloss finishes her work. She packs her **laptop** into her bag. Her classroom is clean and empty. She goes outside. As she walks to her car, she see John and his dad. John's father picks him up with their dog. Mrs. Kloss waves to John and his father.

"Hello, John!" says Mrs. Kloss.

"Good afternoon, Mrs. Kloss," John says.

"Is this the dog that ate your homework?" asks Mrs. Kloss. She smiles, so John knows she is teasing.

"Yes, Mrs. Kloss," says John's father. "Thank you for understanding. John is so worried about getting in trouble!"

Mrs. Kloss is shocked! This time, the dog really did eat the homework.

www.LearnLikeNatives.com

CHAPTER 2
Thrift Store Bargain / house and furniture

HANDLUNG

Louise und Mary sind beste Freundinnen. Sie sind auch **Mitbewohnerinnen**. Sie teilen sich eine **Wohnung** im Zentrum der Stadt. Heute wollen sie **Möbel** für ihr **Zuhause** kaufen. Louise und Mary sind beide Studentinnen. Sie haben nicht viel Geld.

"Wo können wir einkaufen?" fragt Louise Mary.

"Wir brauchen viele Möbel", sagt Mary. Sie macht sich Geldsorgen.

"Ich weiß," sagt Louise. "Wir müssen eine **Schnäppchen** machen."

"Ich habe eine Idee. Lass uns in den Secondhandladen gehen", sagt Mary.

"Gute Idee!" sagt Louise.

Die beiden Mädchen fahren das Auto zum Secondhandladen. Es ist ein riesiger Laden. Das Gebäude ist größer als zehn **Häuser**.

Die Mädchen parken das Auto, der Parkplatz ist leer.

"Toll", sagt Louise. "Der Laden ist sehr groß."

"Total", sagt Mary. "Und hier ist niemand."

www.LearnLikeNatives.com

"Wir werden die Einzigen sein", sagt Louise. "Wir können **es uns gemütlich machen**."

Die Mädchen gehen in den Laden. Der Laden hat alles. Rechts ist der **Küchen**bereich. Es gibt große **Kühlschränke** und alte **Mikrowellen** in den **Regalen**. Es gibt **Toaster** in allen Farben. Die Preise sind gut. Eine Mikrowelle kostet nur 10$.

Alles ist recht günstig. Die Gegenstände sind gebraucht und aus zweiter Hand. Allerdings finden Mary und Louise Gegenstände, die sie mögen. Es gibt mehr als ein Dutzend Sofas. Mary und Louise brauchen ein **Sofa**. Sie verbringen Zeit damit, über die verschiedenen Sofas zu sprechen. Mary mag ein braunes Ledersofa. Louise mag ein großes lila Sofa. Sie können sich nicht einigen. Louise sieht einen lila **Stuhl**. Die Mädchen entscheiden sich für das lila Sofa und den Stuhl, damit sie zusammenpassen. Es ist perfekt für ihr Zuhause.

"Ich brauche ein **Bett** für mein **Schlafzimmer**", sagt Louise.

Die Mädchen gehen zum Schlafbereich. Zuerst passieren sie die Kunstabteilung.

"Wir brauchen etwas für die **Wände**", sagt Louise. Mary stimmt zu. Es gibt große Gemälde, kleine Gemälde, leere **Rahmen** und Fotografien in Rahmen. Louise entscheidet sich für ein großes, abstraktes Gemälde. Es hat Linien von gespritzter roter, blauer und schwarzer Farbe.

"Ich kann so malen", sagt Mary. "Es sieht aus wie ein Kinderbild."

"Es kostet nur fünf Dollar", sagt Louise.

"Ach, okay!" sagt Mary.

Die Mädchen beenden ihren Einkauf. Louise findet auch eine **Lampe** für ihr Schlafzimmer. Ihr Schlafzimmer ist zu dunkel. Mary wählt einen **Teppich** für das **Badezimmer**. Die Mädchen sind sehr glücklich. Sie geben nur 100$ für die gesamte Einrichtung aus.

"Deshalb ist das Einkaufen im Gebrauchtwarenladen ein Schnäppchen", sagt Louise.

"Ja, wir haben **alles Mögliche** eingekauft!" sagt Mary.

www.LearnLikeNatives.com

Mary und Louise haben eine Party in ihrer Wohnung in dieser Nacht. Es ist eine Party, um Freunde willkommen zu heißen. Mary und Louise wollen ihre neuen Möbel zeigen.

Die Türklingel läutet. Mary öffnet die **Tür**. Nick ist der Erste, der ankommt. Nick ist Marys Freund. Nick ist auch Student. Er studiert Kunstgeschichte.

"Hallo, Mädels", sagt Nick: "Danke für die Einladung."

"Komm rein, Nick!" sagt Mary. Nick tritt ins **Foyer** und sie umarmt ihn.

"Willst du unsere neuen Sachen sehen?" fragt Louise.

"Ja!" sagt Nick.

Louise und Mary zeigen Nick die Wohnung. Sie sind glücklich mit dem **Wohnzimmer**. Das neue Sofa, der Stuhl und das Gemälde sehen toll aus.

"All das ist aus dem Gebrauchtwarenladen", sagt Mary. Sie ist stolz.

Nick geht zum Gemälde: "Ich mag dieses Gemälde", sagt er.

"Ich auch", sagt Louise. "Ich habe es gewählt."

"Es erinnert mich an Jackson Pollock", sagt Nick.

"Wer ist Jackson Pollock?" fragt Mary.

"Er ist ein sehr berühmter Maler", sagt Nick. "Er spritzt Farbe auf Leinwände. Genau wie dieses." Nick schaut sich das Gemälde genau an.

"Ist es unterschrieben?" fragt er. Louise schüttelt ihren Kopf. "Dann schauen wir mal dahinter."

Sie nehmen das Bild aus dem Rahmen und drehen es um. Sie sind alle still. Auf der Unterseite befindet sich eine Unterschrift, die wie Jackson Pollocks aussieht.

"Wie viel hast du dafür bezahlt?" fragt Nick.

"Etwa fünf Dollar", sagt Louise.

"Das ist wahrscheinlich mindestens 10 Millionen Dollar wert", sagt Nick. Er ist schockiert. Mary schaut Louise an. Louise schaut Mary an.

www.LearnLikeNatives.com

"Will jemand ein Glas Champagner?", sagt Mary.

Also das ist ein Schnäppchen!

VOKABELLISTE

Mitbewohner	roommates
Wohnung	apartment
Möbel	furniture
Zuhause	home
Schnäppchen	bargain
Secondhandladen	thrift store
Haus	house
es sich gemütlich machen	make ourselves at home
Küche	kitchen
Kühlschränke	refrigerators

Mikrowellen	microwaves
Regale	shelves
Toaster	toasters
Stuhl	chair
Tisch	table
Sofa	sofa
Bett	bed
Schlafzimmer	bedroom
Wand	wall
Rahmen	frame
Lampe	lamp
Teppich	carpet
Badezimmer	bathroom
alles Mögliche	everything but the kitchen sink
Tür	door

www.LearnLikeNatives.com

Foyer	foyer
Wohnzimmer	living room

FRAGEN

1) Warum gehen Mary und Louise in den Gebrauchtwarenladen?

    a) Sie brauchen Geld.

    b) Sie brauchen Möbel, haben aber nicht viel Geld.

    c) Sie haben Möbel zu verkaufen.

    d) Sie wollen Spaß haben.

2) Warum sind die Preise im Gebrauchtwarengeschäft so niedrig?

    a) Es ist Verkaufszeit.

    b) Es schließt.

    c) Die Sachen sind gebraucht.

d) Die Preise sind normal, nicht niedrig.

3) Welche der folgenden Artikel gehört in eine Küche?

    a) Bett

    b) Mikrowelle

    c) Dusche

    d) Sofa

4) Woher weiß Nick so viel über das Gemälde?

    a) Er ist ein professioneller Kunsthändler.

    b) Das Bild gehört Nick.

    c) Er studiert Kunstgeschichte.

    d) Er las ein Buch.

5) Am Ende sind Mary und Louise ...

    a) traurig.

    b) überrascht und reich.

    c) wütend auf Nick.

    d) zu müde für eine Party.

ANTWORTEN

1) Warum gehen Mary und Louise in den Gebrauchtwarenladen?

    b) Sie brauchen Möbel, haben aber nicht viel Geld.

2) Warum sind die Preise im Gebrauchtwarengeschäft so niedrig?

    c) Die Sachen sind gebraucht.

3) Welche der folgenden Artikel gehört in eine Küche?

b) Mikrowelle

4) Woher weiß Nick so viel über das Gemälde?

c) Er studiert Kunstgeschichte.

5) Am Ende sind Mary und Louise...

b) überrascht und reich.

Translation of the Story

Thrift Store Bargain

STORY

Louise and Mary are best friends. They are also **roommates**. They share an **apartment** in the center of town. Today they want to shop for **furniture** for their **home**. Louise and Mary are both students. They do not have much money.

"Where can we shop?" Louise asks Mary.

"We need a lot of furniture," Mary says. She is worried about money.

"I know," says Louise. "We need to find a **bargain**."

"I have an idea. Let's go to the thrift store!" says Mary.

"Great idea!" says Louise.

The two girls drive the car to the thrift store. It is a giant store. The building is bigger than ten **houses**.

The girls park the car. The parking lot is empty.

"Wow," says Louise. "The store is very big."

"Totally," says Mary. "And there is nobody here."

"We will be the only people," says Louise. "We can **make ourselves at home.**"

The girls walk into the store. The store has everything. On the right, there is the **kitchen** section. There are tall **refrigerators** and old **microwaves** on the **shelves**. There are **toasters** of all colors. The prices are good. A microwave costs only $10.

Everything is a bargain. The items are used and second-hand. However, Mary and Louise find items that they like. There are more than a dozen sofas. Mary and Louise need a **sofa**. They spend time talking about the different sofas. Mary likes a brown leather sofa. Louise likes a big purple sofa. They cannot decide. Louise sees a purple **chair**. The girls decide to get the purple sofa and chair so that they match. It is perfect for their home.

"I need a **bed** for my **bedroom**," says Louise.

The girls walk to the bedroom area. First, they pass the art section.

"You know, we need something for the **walls**," says Louise. Mary agrees. There are big paintings, small paintings, empty **frames**, and photographs in frames. Louise decides on a big, abstract painting. It has lines of splattered red, blue, and black paint.

"I can paint like that," says Mary. "It looks like a child's painting."

"It's only five dollars," says Louise.

"Oh, ok!" says Mary.

The girls finish shopping. Louise also finds a **lamp** for her bedroom. Her bedroom is too dark.

Mary chooses a **carpet** for the **bathroom**. The girls are very happy. They spend only $100 dollars for all the furniture.

"That is why shopping at the thrift store is a bargain," says Louise.

"Yes, we got **everything but the kitchen sink**!" says Mary.

Mary and Louise have a party in their apartment that night. It is a party to welcome friends. Mary and Louise want to show their new furniture.

The doorbell rings. Mary opens the **door**. Nick is the first to arrive. Nick is Mary's friend. Nick is also a student. He studies art history.

"Hi, ladies," says Nick. "Thank you for inviting me."

"Come in, Nick!" says Mary. Nick steps into the **foyer**. She hugs him.

"Do you want to see our new stuff?" asks Louise.

"Yeah!" says Nick.

Louise and Mary show Nick around the apartment. They are happy with the **living room**. The new sofa, chair and painting looks great.

"All of this is from the thrift store," says Mary. She is proud.

Nick walks up to the painting. "I really like this painting," he says.

"I do too," says Louise. "I chose it."

"It reminds me of Jackson Pollock," says Nick.

"Who is Jackson Pollock?" asks Mary.

"He is a very famous painter," says Nick. "He splashes paint onto canvas. Just like this one." Nick looks closely at the painting.

"Is it signed?" he asks. Louise shakes her head no. "Let's look behind it then."

They take the painting out of the frame and turn it around. They all are quiet. On the bottom is a signature that looks like 'Jackson Pollock'.

"How much did you pay for this?" asks Nick.

"About five dollars," says Louise.

"This is probably worth at least $10 million dollars," says Nick. He is shocked. Mary looks at Louise. Louise looks at Mary.

"Does anyone want a glass of champagne?" says Mary.

Now that is a bargain!

www.LearnLikeNatives.com

CHAPTER 3
The Goat / common present tense verbs

HANDLUNG

Ollie wacht auf. Die Sonne scheint. Er erinnert sich: Es ist Samstag. Heute **arbeitet** sein Vater nicht. Das bedeutet, Ollie und sein Vater **tun** etwas zusammen. Was können sie tun? Ollie **will** ins Kino gehen. Er will auch Videospiele spielen.

Ollie ist zwölf Jahre alt. Er geht zur Schule. Samstag geht er nicht zur Schule. Er nutzt den Samstag, um zu tun, was er will. Sein Vater lässt ihn entscheiden. Ollie will etwas Lustiges machen.

"Papaaa!" **ruft** Ollie. "**Komm** her!"

Ollie wartet.

Sein Vater betritt Ollies Kinderzimmer.

"Heute ist Samstag", **sagt** Ollie.

"Ich **weiß**, Sohn", sagt Ollies Vater.

"Ich will was Lustiges machen!" sagt Ollie.

"Ich auch", sagt sein Vater.

"Was können wir tun?" **fragt** Ollie.

"Was willst du tun?" fragt sein Vater.

"Ins Kino gehen", sagt Ollie.

"Wir gehen immer am Samstag ins Kino", sagt Ollies Vater.

"Videospiele spielen", sagt Ollie.

"Wir spielen jeden Tag Videospiele", sagt sein Vater.

"Okay, Okay", sagt Ollie. Er **denkt** nach. Er erinnert sich an seinen Lehrer in der Schule. Sein Lehrer **sagt** den Schülern, sie sollen nach draußen gehen. Der Lehrer sagt ihnen, die frische Luft tut ihnen gut. In der Schule lernen sie Tiere kennen. Ollie lernt etwas über Tiere im Dschungel, Tiere im Ozean und Tiere auf Bauernhöfen.

Das ist es, ja! Denkt sich Ollie.

"Papa, lass uns auf einen Bauernhof gehen!" sagt Ollie. Ollies Vater denkt, dass das eine großartige Idee ist. Er wollte schon immer Bauernhoftiere **sehen** und berühren.

Sie nehmen das Auto. Ollies Vater fährt aufs Land. Sie sehen ein Schild, auf dem steht "Tierfarm". Sie folgen den Schildern und parken das Auto.

Ollie und sein Vater kaufen Eintrittskarten. Eintrittskarten kosten 5$. Sie verlassen das Ticketbüro. Es gibt ein großes Holzgebäude, das Bauernhaus. Hinter dem Bauernhaus gibt es ein riesiges Feld. Das Feld hat Bäume, Gras und Zäune. In jedem dieser Zäune befindet sich eine andere Tierart. Es gibt Hunderte von Tieren.

Ollie ist aufgeregt. Er sieht Hühner, Pferde, Enten und Schweine. Er berührt sie und hört ihnen zu. Ollie **macht** bei jedem Tier einen Laut. Zu den

Enten sagt er "quak". Zu den Schweinen sagt er "quiek" . Zu den Pferden sagt er "wieher" zu den Hühnern, sagt er "gack, gack". Die Tiere starren Ollie an.

Vorbei an den Tieren in Käfigen sieht Ollie eine Schafsherde. Ollies Vater erzählt ihm, dass weibliche Schafe Auen genannt werden. Männliche Schafe sind Widder. Babyschafe heißen Lämmer. Schafe fressen Gras.

"Sie können uns sehen", sagt sein Vater.

"Aber sie sehen uns nicht an", sagt Ollie.

"Schafe können hinter sich sehen. Sie müssen ihre Köpfe nicht bewegen", sagt sein Vater. Ollies Vater weiß eine Menge über Schafe.

"Im Frühling schneiden sie den Schafen die Haare ab", sagt sein Vater. Er erzählt Ollie, wie die Schafwolle zu Pullover, Schals und anderen warmen Kleidungsstücken **wird**. Ollie hat einen Pullover aus Wolle, er ist warm.

Ollie und sein Vater gehen auf das Feld. Das Gras ist grün. Es gibt Kühe in einer Ecke. Eine der Mutterkühe ernährt ein Kälbchen.

"Weißt du, was Kühe machen, Ollie?" fragt sein Vater.

"Man! Milch!" sagt Ollie.

"Das ist richtig", sagt sein Vater.

Ollie hört ein Tierlaut. Er **nimmt** die Hand seines Vaters. Sie gehen auf das Geräusch zu. Sie kommen zu einem Zaun. Sie **finden** eine Ziege. Die Ziege steckt mit den Hörnern im Zaun fest. Die Ziege sitzt auf dem Boden. Sie bewegt sich nicht. Ihre Hörner stecken zwischen dem Holz und sie kann sich nicht bewegen. Ollie und sein Vater **schauen** die Ziege an.

"Die Ziege tut mir so leid", sagt Ollie. Sie scheint traurig.

"Armer Kerl!" sagt sein Vater.

"Er sieht so traurig aus", sagt Ollie.

"Wir können ihm helfen", sagt sein Vater.

"Ja!" sagt Ollie.

Sie nähern sich der Ziege. Ollie ist nervös. Papa sagt, man soll sich keine Sorgen machen. Die Hörner stecken fest und die Ziege wird ihnen nicht wehtun. Ollie blickt der Ziege in die Augen. Die Ziege **braucht** Hilfe. Ollie spricht mit der Ziege. Er **versucht** sanfte Töne zu machen. Er will die Ziege ruhig halten.

Ollies Vater versucht, die Hörner zu bewegen. Erst das rechte Horn, dann das linke Horn. Sie bewegen sich nicht. Nach zehn Minuten **geben** sie **auf**.

"Ich kann es nicht tun", sagt Ollies Vater.

"Bist du sicher?" fragt Ollie.

"Die Hörner stecken fest", sagt sein Vater.

"Was machen wir?" fragt Ollie.

Der Bereich um die Ziege ist schlammig. Es ist kein Gras mehr übrig. Ollies Vater nimmt etwas Gras vom Boden und bringt es zur Ziege. Die Ziege frisst das Gras. Die Ziege sieht hungrig aus. Das Gras ist weg. Ollie bekommt mehr Gras für die Ziege. Sie streicheln die Ziege für ein paar Minuten. Die Ziege scheint dankbar zu sein.

"Sagen wir es dem Besitzer", sagt sein Vater.

"Ja", sagt Ollie, "vielleicht kann er ihr helfen."

Ollie und sein Vater gehen zum Ticketbüro. Das Ticketbüro ist ein kleines Gebäude am Eingang. Ein Mann arbeitet dort. Ollie und sein Vater gehen rein.

"Hallo, der Herr", sagt Ollies Vater.

"Wie kann ich Ihnen helfen?" fragt der Mann.

"Da ist eine Ziege ...", sagt Ollies Vater.

Der Mann unterbricht Ollies Vater. Er winkt mit der Hand. Er sieht gelangweilt aus. "Ja, wissen wir."

"Sie wissen von der Ziege?" fragt Ollie.

"Die Ziege die im Zaun feststeckt?" fragt der Mann.

"Ja!" sagen Ollie und sein Vater.

"Oh ja, das ist Patty", sagt der Mann. "Sie kann sich frei bewegen, wann immer sie will. Sie mag nur die Aufmerksamkeit."

Ollie **gibt** seinem Vater einen überraschten Blick. Ollie und sein Vater lachen.

"Patty, was für eine Ziege!" sagt Ollie.

ZUSAMMENFASSUNG

Ollie wacht an einem Samstag auf. Er und sein Vater entscheiden, etwas Lustiges zu tun. Sie gehen auf einen Bauernhof, um Tiere zu sehen. Sie sehen und berühren viele Tiere: Kühe, Pferde, Schafe und mehr. Sie laufen auf dem Bauernhof herum. Es ist ein schöner Tag. Sie finden eine in einem Zaun eingeklemmte Ziege. Sie versuchen, der Ziege zu helfen. Die Ziege steckt mit den

Hörnern fest. Sie füttern sie mit Gras. Ollie und sein Vater holen Hilfe. Der Mann im Ticketbüro hört ihnen zu. Er erzählt ihnen, dass die Ziege die Leute gerne hereinlegt, um Aufmerksamkeit zu erhalten. Ollie und sein Vater lachen.

VOKABELLISTE

arbeiten	to work
tun	to do
wollen	to want
gehen	to go
benutzen	to use
rufen	to call
kommen	to come
sagen	to say
wissen	to know
fragen	to ask
denken	to think

www.LearnLikeNatives.com

erzählen	to tell
sehen	to see
werden	to become
machen	to make
nehmen	to take
finden	to find
fühlen	to feel
schauen	to look
bekommen	to get
brauchen	to need
versuchen	to try
geben	to give

FRAGEN

1) Was machen Ollie und sein Vater am Samstag?

www.LearnLikeNatives.com

    a) ins Kino gehen

    b) auf einen Bauernhof gehen

    c) Videospiele spielen

    d) zur Schule gehen

2) Über welches Tier weiß Ollies Vater viel?

    a) Schaf

    b) Schwein

    c) Giraffe

    d) Kuh

3) Was passiert mit der Ziege?

    a) es versteckt sich

    b) es frisst

    c) es steckt fest

    d) es ist wütend

www.LearnLikeNatives.com

4) Was tun Ollie und sein Vater für die Ziege?

    a) sie befreien

    b) Gras geben und streicheln

    c) die Polizei anrufen

    d) sie küssen

.

5) Was macht Patty?

    a) sie verlässt den Hof

    b) sie isst Müll

    c) sie geht zum Ticketbüro

    d) so tun als würde sie feststeckte, um Aufmerksamkeit zu bekommen

ANTWORTEN

1) Was machen Ollie und sein Vater am Samstag?

b) auf einen Bauernhof gehen

2) Über welches Tier weiß Ollies Vater viel?

a) Schaf

3) Was passiert mit der Ziege?

c) es steckt fest

4) Was tun Ollie und sein Vater für die Ziege?

b) Gras geben und streicheln

5) Was macht Patty?

d) so tun als würde sie feststeckte, um Aufmerksamkeit zu bekommen

www.LearnLikeNatives.com

Translation of the Story

The Goat

Ollie wakes up. The sun is shining. He remembers: it is Saturday. Today his dad does not **work**. That means Ollie and his dad **do** something together. What can they do? Ollie **wants** to go to the movies. He also wants to play video games.

Ollie is twelve years old. He goes to school. Saturday he does not go to school. He **uses** Saturday to do what he wants. His dad lets him decide. So Ollie wants to do something fun.

"Daaaaaad!" **calls** Ollie. "**Come** here!"

Ollie waits.

His dad enters Ollie's bedroom.

"Today is Saturday," **says** Ollie.

"I **know**, son," says Ollie's dad.

"I want to do something fun!" says Ollie.

"Me too," says Dad.

"What can we do?" **asks** Ollie.

"What do you want to do?" asks his dad.

"Go to the movies," says Ollie.

"We always go to the movies on Saturday," says Ollie's dad.

"Play video games," says Ollie.

"We play video games everyday!" says Dad.

"Ok, ok," says Ollie. He **thinks**. He remembers his teacher at school. His teacher **tells** the students to go outside. The teacher tells them the fresh air is good. At school, they study animals. Ollie learns about animals in the jungle, animals in the ocean, and animals on farms.

That's it!

"Dad, let's go to a farm!" says Ollie. Ollie's dad thinks that is a great idea. He has always wanted to **see** and touch farm animals.

They take the car. Ollie's dad drives to the countryside. They see a sign that says "Animal Farm". They follow the signs and park the car.

Ollie and his dad buy tickets to enter. Tickets cost $5. They leave the ticket office. There is a big wooden building, the farmhouse. Behind the farmhouse, there is a huge field. The field has trees, grass, and fences. In each fence is a different type of animal. There are hundreds of animals.

Ollie is excited. He sees chickens, horses, ducks, and pigs. He touches them and listens to them. Ollie **makes** a sound to each animal. To the ducks, he says "quack". To the pigs, he says "oink". To the horses, he says "nay". To the chickens, he says "bok bok". The animals stare at Ollie.

Past the animals in cages, Ollie sees a flock of sheep. Ollie's dad tells him that female sheep are called ewes. Male sheep are rams. Baby sheep are called lambs. The sheep are eating grass.

"They can see us," says Dad.

"But they are not looking at us," says Ollie.

"Sheep can see behind themselves. They don't have to turn their heads," says Dad. Ollie's dad knows a lot about sheep.

"They cut the hair on the sheep in spring," says Dad. He tells Ollie how the sheep's wool **becomes** sweaters, scarves and other warm clothing. Ollie has a sweater made of wool. It is warm.

Ollie and his dad walk around the field. The grass is green. There are cows in a corner. One of the mother cows feeds a baby calf.

"You know what cows make, Ollie?" asks Dad.

"Duh! Milk!" says Ollie.

"That's right," says Dad.

Ollie hears an animal sound. He **takes** his dad's hand. They walk towards the sound. They come to a fence. They **find** a goat. The goat has horns stuck in the fence. The goat sits on the ground. It does not move. Its horns are between the wood and it can't move. Ollie and his dad **look** at the goat.

"I feel so bad for the goat," says Ollie. She seems sad.

"Poor guy!" says Dad.

"He looks so sad," says Ollie.

"We can help him," Dad says.

"Yeah!" says Ollie.

They get close to the goat. Ollie is nervous. Dad says not to worry. The horns are stuck and the goat will not hurt them. Ollie looks into the eyes of the goat. The goat **needs** help. Ollie talks to the goat. He **tries** to make soft sounds. He wants to keep the goat calm.

Ollie's dad tries to move the horns. He tries the right horn. He tries the left horn. They don't move. After ten minutes, they **give up**.

"I can't do it," says Ollie's dad.

"Are you sure?" asks Ollie.

"The horns are stuck," says Dad.

"What do we do?" asks Ollie.

The area around the goat is mud. There is no grass left. Ollie's dad takes some grass from the ground and brings it to the goat. The goat eats the grass. The goat looks hungry. The grass is gone. Ollie gets more grass to take to the goat. They pet the goat for a few minutes. The goat seems grateful.

"Let's tell the owner," says Dad.

"Yeah," says Ollie. "Maybe they can help her."

Ollie and his dad go to the ticket office. The ticket office is a small building at the entrance. A man works there. Ollie and his dad go inside.

"Hello, sir," says Ollie's dad.

"How can I help you?" asks the man.

"There's a goat—" says Ollie's dad.

The man interrupts Ollie's dad. He waves his hand. He looks bored. "Yeah, we know."

"You know about the goat?" asks Ollie.

"The goat stuck in the fence?" asks the man.

"Yes!" say Ollie and his dad.

"Oh yes, that's Patty," says the man. "She can get herself out whenever she wants. She just likes the attention."

Ollie **gives** his dad a surprised look. Ollie and his dad laugh.

"Patty, what a goat!" Ollie says.

CONCLUSION

You did it!

You finished a whole book in a brand new language. That in and of itself is quite the accomplishment, isn't it?

Congratulate yourself on time well spent and a job well done. Now that you've finished the book, you have familiarized yourself with over 500 new vocabulary words, comprehended the heart of 3 short stories, and listened to loads of dialogue unfold, all without going anywhere!

Charlemagne said "To have another language is to possess a second soul." After immersing yourself in this book, you are broadening your horizons and opening a whole new path for yourself.

Have you thought about how much you know now that you did not know before? You've learned everything from how to greet and how to express your emotions to basics like colors and place words. You can tell time and ask question. All without opening a schoolbook. Instead, you've cruised through fun, interesting stories and possibly listened to them as well.

Perhaps before you weren't able to distinguish meaning when you listened to German. If you used the audiobook, we bet you can now pick out meanings and words when you hear someone speaking. Regardless, we are sure you have taken an important step to being more fluent. You are well on your way!

Best of all, you have made the essential step of distinguishing in your mind the idea that most often hinders people studying a new language. By approaching German through our short stories and dialogs, instead of formal lessons with just grammar and vocabulary, you are no longer in the 'learning' mindset. Your approach is much more similar to an osmosis, focused on speaking and using the language, which is the end goal, after all!

So, what's next?

This is just the first of five books, all packed full of short stories and dialogs, covering essential, everyday German that will ensure you master the basics. You can find the rest of the books in the series, as well as a whole host of other resources, at LearnLikeNatives.com. Simply add the book to your library to take the next step in your language learning journey. If you are ever in need of new ideas or direction, refer to our 'Speak Like a Native' eBook, available to you for free at LearnLikeNatives.com, which clearly outlines practical steps you can take to continue learning any language you choose.

www.LearnLikeNatives.com

We also encourage you to get out into the real world and practice your German. You have a leg up on most beginners, after all—instead of pure textbook learning, you have been absorbing the sound and soul of the language. Do not underestimate the foundation you have built reviewing the chapters of this book. Remember, no one feels 100% confident when they speak with a native speaker in another language.

One of the coolest things about being human is connecting with others. Communicating with someone in their own language is a wonderful gift. Knowing the language turns you into a local and opens up your world. You will see the reward of learning languages for many years to come, so keep that practice up!. Don't let your fears stop you from taking the chance to use your German. Just give it a try, and remember that you will make mistakes. However, these mistakes will teach you so much, so view every single one as a small victory! Learning is growth.

www.LearnLikeNatives.com

Don't let the quest for learning end here! There is so much you can do to continue the learning process in an organic way, like you did with this book. Add another book from Learn Like a Native to your library. Listen to German talk radio. Watch some of the great German Musical. Put on the latest CD from Sarah Connor. Take cooking lessons in German. Whatever you do, don't stop because every little step you take counts towards learning a new language, culture, and way of communicating.

www.LearnLikeNatives.com

www.LearnLikeNatives.com

www.LearnLikeNatives.com

Learn Like a Native is a revolutionary **language education brand** that is taking the linguistic world by storm. Forget boring grammar books that never get you anywhere, Learn Like a Native teaches you languages in a fast and fun way that actually works!

As an international, multichannel, language learning platform, we provide **books, audio guides and eBooks** so that you can acquire the knowledge you need, swiftly and easily.

Our **subject-based learning**, structured around real-world scenarios, builds your conversational muscle and ensures you learn the content most relevant to your requirements. Discover our tools at ***LearnLikeNatives.com***.

When it comes to learning languages, we've got you covered!

www.ingramcontent.com/pod-product-compliance
Lightning Source LLC
Chambersburg PA
CBHW062052280426
43661CB00088B/719